CRUSH SCHOOL

EVERY STUDENT'S GUIDE TO KILLING IT IN THE CLASSROOM

(AND TEACHERS DIG IT TOO)

By Oskar Cymerman
Focus 2 Achieve | focus2achieve.com

WHAT OTHERS ARE SAYING...

"I found myself smiling all through this book! The author has the most wonderful attitude, and I adore the way he's 'talking' to the kids. It feels like he's having a conversation with them. To me, that's always the best kind of writing. I absolutely think the book will be helpful. The author clearly knows his stuff and audience. They'll be able to feel his authenticity, wisdom, and caring."

- Rae Pica, Author/Radio Host/Co-founder of BAM! Radio Network

"I think kids would enjoy this book, because it has humor and you don't have to read the whole thing. Most kids just want to go to the part of the book they need and that's how 'Crush School' is supposed to be used. I liked that the author understands what kids go through and has experiences working with kids. He's not this rich billionaire, but someone who is just talking to you and trying to help you."

- Bailey Harper, 5th Grade Student

"I am a huge fan! I love the conversational style. I love that the casual language keeps it very real, but it doesn't sound forced, either. 'Crush School' is a perfect balance between solid research, concepts, and strategies along with examples, analogies, and humor. The messages are realistic and feel "doable" for the reader. The chapters are brief and to the point and hit on many aspects of successful learning. Amazing!"

- Lisa Hyland, Student Achievement Specialist/AVID Coordinator

"Learning how to learn is critical to helping all students succeed. 'Crush School' tells students exactly what they need to know and presents it in a way that students are far more likely to read it and apply. A book that every student would benefit from using."

- Nancy Weinstein, Founder and CEO of Mindprint Learning

"Great book. I would have my middle schoolers read it. I like the the tone of the book. The organizers and tips are awesome. I like that the author uses high level language. Usually, the authors water down language to appeal to readers. I think that if we expect the kids to understand the demanding academic lexicon they need to be exposed to it. No excuses after learning that their brain CAN learn!"

- Anna Janicki, K-8 Teacher/ELL Instructor

I DEDICATE THIS BOOK TO...

All Students Everywhere In The Universe: I didn't find room for vampires in this book, but I did include a couple of lines about zombies. I hope you like them.

My Son Adam: When you came into this world 2 ½ years ago, you helped me realize how much I love life and people. I learn from you everyday. You're the bomb! I love you and I hope to one day become half the man you are.

My Wife Kasia: I'm finally done with this thing! Thank you for making it easy to know what's most important in life. I love you and we can go on vacation now. How about a tent, mosquitoes, and a 2 ½ year old?

Matt Damon: I need someone to write the Foreword for this thing and Oprah wasn't available. What say you brother?

FOREWORD

A little over a year ago, I was sitting on the couch late at night playing online poker. I love Texas Hold'em. I'm good at it. So good in fact, that in a few short months, I won 170,000,000 in fake chips starting at a mere 800.

How did I do it?

I played, learned, and played some more. I played a lot. I collected more and more fake chips; an undeniable proof of my learning and skill. As I learned to play, I also learned to anticipate events by reflecting on how some hands went down. Then, I applied what I learned in the future hands.

In some cases, I knew I was doing it. In many, I had not a clue.

School is the same way. To get good at school, you have to learn, practice, and apply what you learn. You have to do it a lot too. To get really good at it, you must reflect and become aware of how you learn. And to be an absolute learning machine? Use this book.

I did not say "Read this book" for a reason. You see, my poker addiction did not lead to a fortune. But the game taught me something. I know now, that if I learn to use my brain the right way, I can learn anything I want. And so can you. So I stopped playing poker and wrote this book instead.

USE IT AT YOUR OWN RISK.

Table of Contents

Yo!

If you were looking for a boy meets girl novel – this ain't it. Wrong kind of crush if you know what I mean. Sucker!

I know. This isn't how most books start. But this isn't most books. For one, this book is SHORT. Straight and to the point. It is not meant to put you to sleep while you're trying to figure out HOW TO CRUSH SCHOOL.

Yes, this book is about KILLING IT – getting to the lightbulb moments – LEARNING ANYTHING.

SO WHO IS THIS BOOK FOR?

If you suck at school – this book is for you. If you experience average success at school – this book is for you. If you do well at school – this book is for you. IF YOU ARE A STUDENT – THIS BOOK IS FOR YOU. It does not matter if you're a middle school, high school, or college student – this book is for you.

If you apply the things you learn as you read, you will become a better student regardless of how good or bad at school you are right now.

That's a threat, not a promise.

This English dude named Herbert Spencer once said that *"the great aim of education is not knowledge but action."* In the same vein, this book is a promise:

IF YOU DO THE WORK, YOU WILL GET RESULTS.

But, if you read it, and take no action, then you might as well have thrown your money down the toilet and spend your time staring at a wall, because knowledge is not power. It is only potential for power. To possess knowledge and not to use it is the same as not having it at all. Just more useless brain cells.

IF YOU READ THIS BOOK AND DON'T APPLY THE KNOWLEDGE IT DROPS ON YOU NOTHING WILL CHANGE.

If are you ready to become a better student this book will take you there. But you have to commit. No punking out now.

SIGN THE PLEDGE.

I _____ pledge, with the Universe as my witness, that I will read this book and use the strategies it contains.

Are you ready? Let's Crush School.

CHAPTER 1 - HOW DOES THIS THING WORK?

This book is short for one main reason: I want you to read it. To change things and be more successful, you have to read it and implement its knowledge.

Keeping this book short was probably the hardest thing about writing it. I did not want to waste your time with snooze stories, but I felt I needed to tell you the truth and explain why the strategies I included here work. I want them to make sense, so that you do them.

If you like this book, that's awesome. But I want you to know that I'm not in it for the cheers. I mean, cheerleaders are awesome. Except maybe when they break up with you right before the homecoming dance. Or during. Besides, while cheerleading is fun, it's a short-lived gig.

And this world desperately needs more innovators, creatives, and game changers.

IT NEEDS YOU ON YOUR A-GAME.

Accomplishing that is no small task. So let's get going!

 HOW YOU READ MATTERS.

Read actively. That means that you should take notes while you read THIS OR ANY OTHER PIECE OF TEXT, highlight, circle, underline etc. Your brain makes stronger connections, so you understand and remember better when you read actively.

If you are holding a printed copy of the book go to page 63 for tips on how to use this book.

If you are using an e-Device to read you can:

1. Print it and mark it up using my tips.

or

2. Download a free app such as Adobe Reader for iPad or Android and use my tips to mark up the PDF copy of this book.

IF YOU DON'T DO THIS YOU WON'T BE AS EFFECTIVE.

This is not a romance novel, so

FEEL FREE TO SKIP AROUND.

In fact, you should skip around and use sections that can help you right when you need the info they possess. Do it!

To make sure that you use it and to get the most use out of this book

HAVE IT WITH YOU AT HOME AND SCHOOL.

Have it in your pack, purse, phone/tablet. It will help you learn wherever you are. It helps in all subjects, because the tips it contains help you become a better learner. And guess what?

YOU LEARN EVERYWHERE ALL THE TIME.

CHAPTER 2 –
CHANGE YOUR MIND, CHANGE YOUR LIFE.

"But I'm not a Math person."

"I've never been good at Science."

"I can't write well to get a good grade in English."

Sound familiar? Of course it does. If you have not said something similar in the past, your friends have.

If you tell yourself that you can't do something before you try it, you will sure enough fail at it. This is because you're communicating to your brain that something is impossible. In return, your brain believes you and does everything in its power to prove you correct. It sabotages your progress!

But you know what? I told you I will be honest with you. So:

STOP MAKING EXCUSES.

Yes. Some classes are tough.

And yes, some teachers suck.

And then, some things seem impossible right up until the moment you do them.

Think about it. There were things in your life you thought you'd never accomplish. But you did. Think back. Remember? Why should school be any different?

Attitude is everything… So work on changing yours for the better.

Or don't. YOUR CHOICE. Just remember this:

YOU ARE THE ONLY PERSON WHO CAN STOP YOU.

CHAPTER 3 - THE LEARNING STYLES MYTH

"I'm visual."

"I learn better by doing stuff."

Have you ever taken a test that decided you learn best in a certain style? If you have, the results told you that you learn best by seeing, hearing, reading/writing, or doing. But guess what?

IT'S A BUNCH OF DOO-DOO.

What?!?! That's right. You may prefer watching videos to reading books or hearing others talk. That's cool. All I'm saying is that you (and everybody else) learn in many different ways. Even more than those 4 mentioned above.

Believing in this poop-of-a-theory can be harmful. When you start focusing on one mode of receiving information you miss out on using all of your brain power. The brain is at its best when it gets the info in multiple ways. That's why we have ears, eyes, tongue, hands, and nerves.

Don't taste books though. That's weird. Don't be weird.

What if you tell your teachers or counselors that the learning styles theory is a myth and they don't believe you?

Don't argue with them. I don't want you to get in trouble.

Just have them call me: 651-757-6635 - that's my REAL cell phone number.

Seriously. I have a ton of rollover minutes and no clue what to do with them. I got you.

CHAPTER 4 - YOUR AWESOME BRAIN

"The human brain has 100 billion neurons, each neuron connected to 10 thousand other neurons. Sitting on your shoulders is the most complicated object in the known universe." - Michio Kaku

WARNING! This part will be a little heavy on neuroscience, but it is important that I talk about what happens in your brain so you believe that YOU CAN LEARN ANYTHING.

If after reading this part you see it as nerdy gibberish than you are probably correct. After all, I specialize in nerdy sciency things.

But before you completely dismiss it know this:

I AM YOUR FATHER.

Okay. That's a lie. But still… Take a brief look at neurons and synapses on the next page, because I want you to know how great your brain is and what it does.

YOUR BRAIN IS AWESOME.

IT DOES AMAZING THINGS.

MAKES SENSE OUT OF NONSENSE.

EVEN GIBBERISH

BUT YOU MUST GIVE IT A CHANCE.

Each brain cell or neuron you own has 2 main parts:
cell body and axon. The cell body is the orange
part with tentacles (kinda) called dendrites and
axon is the red tail that also ends in tentacles
(blue) called axon tips or terminals.

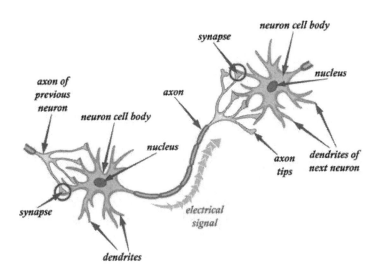

A synapse forms when axon tips of one neuron meet the dendrites of another neuron. When you are learning new concepts, new synapses form. Because the information is new the connections are weak at first.

Thus, the key to becoming an expert, a Jedi master at science, math, spelling, writing etc. is using the new information so the connections can become strong.

And, it matters when, where, how, and how often you use it. The more you do with the information the better you remember and understand it.

You see, the brain is a use it or lose it organ that needs time to strengthen new connections. Let it.

CHAPTER 5 – 2 MODES OF THINKING

That thing between your ears is a powerful tool.

Even if you don't believe it right now:

YOUR BRAIN CAN MASTER SUPER DIFFICULT CONCEPTS.

Let me show you how. First, you need to find out about the 2 distinct thinking modes your brain operates in: focused mode and diffuse mode.

THE FOCUSED MODE

Your brain is in the Focused Mode when you are FOCUSING on the information you are learning. You might be reading, solving a problem, taking a test etc.

Why is it important?

This is the mode in which your understanding of a concept begins to form. As you recall and practice the concept in focused mode you master it.

THE DIFFUSE MODE

Your brain is in the Diffuse Mode when you are RELAXING. You might be sleeping, napping, daydreaming, playing, walking, chatting.

Why is it important?

This is the mode in which your unconscious mind is working on concepts without you knowing it. Your brain cells (neurons) are making and strengthening connections between information.

FOCUSED AND DIFFUSE MODE FACTS

1. You are either in the focused or diffuse mode of thinking, but not both at the same time.

2. The diffuse mode allows you to look at concepts from new perspectives and make connections our brain is unaware of in the focused mode.

3. To best absorb and master information YOUR MIND NEEDS TO ALTERNATE BETWEEN THE FOCUSED AND DIFFUSE MODES.

Here's the way of the warrior you can follow to learn it all:

#1	**#2**	**#3**	**#4**
FOCUS & AVOID DISTRACTIONS when learning a concept the first time.	STEP AWAY from the new info or problem. Take a break and relax. Sleep on it. Make sure you get enough sleep.	Don't Give Up! Come back to it later or the next day. FOCUS again. Sooner or later IT WILL CLICK.	ALTERNATE this practice of FOCUSING and RELAXING over several days/weeks.

BOTTOM LINE:

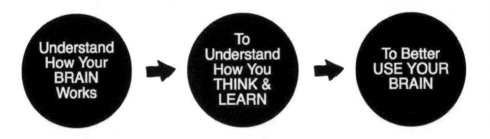

DO THIS TO GET TOUGH STUFF AND BECOME A BETTER LEARNER.

CHAPTER 6 - MEMORY

"What we process, we learn. If we are not processing life, we're not living it. Live life."

— Peter Doolittle

Memories are what life is made of. You make memories when your brain processes the information you receive. The more times you process, the stronger the neural connections, the better you remember.

There are 2 kinds of memory:

WORKING MEMORY	LONG-TERM MEMORY
1. Stores immediate experiences and knowledge. 2. Is used to pull out long term memory. 3. Manipulates current ideas and memories. 4. Is brief: holds information for about 20 seconds if not used.	1. Stores information over a long period of time. 2. Is seemingly capable of storing unlimited amount of data.

They are both important. Working memory is what helps you be a good listener, absorb information, and think on your feet. Long-term memory is what helps you recall facts and events from the past, so you can use them in the present.

What I'm saying is this:

WORKING MEMORY IS LIMITED SO YOU NEED TO LEARN HOW TO MOVE INFORMATION FROM WORKING TO LONG-TERM MEMORY EFFECTIVELY.

Let me show you how.

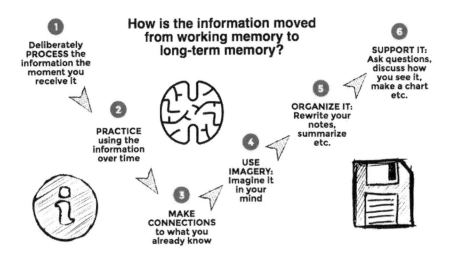

The message in the picture above is this:

THE MORE STUFF YOU DO WITH THE INFORMATION YOU'RE LEARNING, THE BETTER YOU REMEMBER IT.

Now you know why your teachers always say:
"Practice Makes Permanent!" But it's not just any
practice. Here's the

CRUSH SCHOOL! APPROACH:

1. Get Good Sleep (Chapter 9).
2. Use The KISS Method (Chapter 10).
3. Focus (Chapter 11 and Chapter 16).
4. Space It Out (Chapter 17).
5. Mix It Up (Chapter 19).

Don't worry.

We'll get there.

Just keep going.

CHAPTER 7 - HABITS

Habits are things you do automatically. Many habits are good. You'd go nuts if you had to think about every little thing in your day. So, your brain does them in the background.

Brushing your teeth is a good example. At this point in your life, you don't think about it consciously. You just do it. Most of the time you don't even remember the ins and outs tooth brushing. You know how, but don't think about it any more. You just brush and done. It's a habit.

Some habits are not so good. And, they are hard to break. Your teachers and parental units are on your case to STOP IT, whatever IT is. You try. Not happening. You tell yourself you will not procrastinate this time around. Then you do. You have the best intentions. I know. You know. But your brain doesn't care. It does it's own thing.

You have to train your brain.

This book will show you how.

TAKE A GOOD HARD LOOK AT YOUR HABITS.

❏ Poor Sleep: Do I get enough hours of sleep each night?

❏ Procrastination: Do I put off what I know I need to get done?

❏ Distractions: Do I multitask and slow myself down?

❏ Lack of Grit: Do I give up too quickly?

❏ Passive Learning: Do I expect to learn - simply 'cause I'm at my desk?

❏ Unproductive: Am I as productive as I could be in class?

❏

❏

For now, just read through the habits above and think about which ones affect you the most. I will talk about them all in detail and help you improve.

Are there any other habits you can add to the list? If so, add them as 7 and 8, because guess what:

I WILL TALK ABOUT THEM IN THIS BOOK.

That's right. I'm psychic.

ACTIONS:

1. Put a checkmark next to each habit listed on the previous page that you feel you could change or improve.
2. If you are ready, pick and underline the one you want to start changing RIGHT NOW.
3. Read the next chapter "Train Your Brain."
4. Go to the section of the book related to your bad habit, read it, and work your plan.

CHAPTER 8 - TRAIN YOUR BRAIN

Your brain's #1 job is to help you survive, so it often refuses spending energy on other things. Especially things it perceives as risky.

Change can be risky. Even if the change is reasonable, your brain often sees it as risky. And, it might resist it. So, you gotta make your brain do it. Over and over.

Being afraid of change or resisting to leave our comfort zone is pretty normal. Everyone experiences these feelings at some point in their life. Such behavior can often be explained as a brain habit developed over the course of human progress. As we became more comfortable, we became more constricted.

Habits are basically connected brain neurons. The more established the habit, the stronger the connections. To drop a bad habit, you need to weaken those connections. To develop a good habit, you need to form and strengthen new ones. How?

REPLACE A BAD HABIT WITH A GOOD ONE.

Here's the "Make It Easy, Take It Easy" way:

1. **MAKE IT EASY.** It's always hardest to start something. So start slow. Say you cram before tests and would like to be more consistent. Instead of telling yourself that you'll just stop it, devote just 5 minutes to study each day. Just 5 flipping minutes! Set your phone to alert you **every single day** at the same time and do it.

2. **TAKE IT EASY.** Once you get going, keep going and keep adding an extra minute or two each week. Careful though! **Do not try to go from 5 minutes to 30 minutes right away.** Doing that might stress your brain out and you might go back to the old behavior.

When you use the "Make It Easy, Take It Easy" way to form new good habits your self-esteem will grow. This is because you will experience success in reaching goals. And it really doesn't matter how small the goals are.

GAINING MOMENTUM IS THE KEY.

You might feel that the goal is so small that it's silly…

That's awesome! It means that it will take a small effort to perform. And, you'll be able to add a few more tiny goals like this one to your daily routine.

Check this out:

Your teacher assigns a chapter to read. You know you should, but it's just too much, so you don't. What if you just read one page today, one tomorrow, and one each and every day after that? It's easy! It will take only a few minutes and then you can go on with your life. In a week, you'll have 7 pages read. Even if the chapter consisted of 10 pages, you read more than you normally would have and you are developing a good habit. That's easy, isn't it?

$$1+2+3+4=10$$

Forming new habits the "Make It Easy, Take It Easy" way will also build up your willpower to do the right thing. When the task or project seems huge, your brain stresses out and goes back to the old behavior, so break it up into tiny pieces.

ACTIONS:

1. Write your tiny goals out and put them somewhere you will see them often like the fridge door.
2. Put alerts in your phone that remind you to perform the action you're supposed to do.
3. Recording the tasks, however tiny they are, starts training your brain to do them and rewiring it for action.

Make it easy. Take it easy. Train your brain. You got this!

CHAPTER 9 — SLEEP IS LIKE REALLY GOOD

This Just In:

YOUR MIND IS A TOXIC CESSPOOL.

There I've said it:

YOUR MIND IS TOXIC.

Please forgive my honesty, but it's the truth. It's because you don't sleep enough.

You see, your brain uses like 20% of all your energy, which is pretty amazing considering it's not that huge compared to the rest of you. I'm not saying your butt looks big in those skinny jeans, but it's bigger than your brain and uses a lot less energy.

Because your brain uses so much energy, the brain cells produce a lot of waste products. This waste is made up of toxins that can destroy brain cells unless they are removed. The buildup of toxins makes it hard for you to focus. Because a tired brain doesn't work as well, learning is harder.

Here's what happens again:

Toxins
Toxins
Everywhere

*"Insane In The Membrane
Insane In The Brain"*

Being awake
produces

metabolic toxins!!!

in your brain.

These toxins impair
your brain's ability
to operate at its full
potential. You don't
learn as well, your
focus suffers, and
you can't create
and communicate
as effectively.

If you do not
sleep enough,
your brain
cannot get rid of
the toxins and,
whether you
realize it or not,
you continue to
underperform.

But there's the good news:

YOUR BRAIN IS SIMILAR TO A DISHWASHER.

The metabolic toxins in the brain get flushed out
by brain fluid when we sleep. During sleep, your
brain cells rest and shrink to allow the fluid to
flow in between and flush out the toxins. That can
only happen when you sleep enough.

The reasons I have just given should be enough for
you to want to improve your sleeping habits, but
just in case let me tell you a couple more things…

Hopefully, dropping all this knowledge on you will
smack some serious sense into you!

SLEEP TO BECOME AWESOMER (BETTER, STRONGER, FASTER).

Check out what happens when you get good sleep:

In case you are still not convinced that you should sleep more, check out the reasons below, and learn how you can use sleep to become better at learning.

1. Sleep = Better Memory Formation
   - Your brain organizes ideas & concepts you are learning while you sleep.
   - Your brain rehearses information as you sleep.
   - Less important info is erased.

2. Sleep = Improved Problem Solving
   - When you turn the "conscious" off, other parts of your brain "talk" and make connections between concepts you're learning.

3. Study Before Nap/Bed
   - This increases the chances of dreaming about what you are learning.
   - Dreaming about the concepts you are learning improves your ability to understand them as your brain forms stronger neural connections.

YOU LITERALLY GET SMARTER AS YOU SNOOZE!

SO HOW MUCH SLEEP DO WE NEED?

- 5-12 year olds need 10-11 hours of sleep.
- 12-18 year olds need 8.5-10 hours of sleep.
- Adults need 7.5-9 hours of sleep.

I must admit, the poor sleep habit is a hard one to change. I struggle with it myself.

Just remember this:

1. A tired brain is full of toxins that mess with your ability to think clearly and be productive.
2. These toxins are also tied to dementia and Alzheimer's.
3. Number 1 and 2 above really suck.

ACTION:

If you consistently do not get enough sleep:

1. Start by going to bed 5 minutes earlier each night.
2. Decide which time you want to go to sleep and set an alarm on your phone 15 minutes prior so you can brush your teeth, text your BF/GF/BFF etc.
3. GO TO SLEEP. NOW.

CHAPTER 10 – THE KISS METHOD

Keep It Simple Stupid! That's what my favorite teacher in High School, Mr. Dennis used to say. Besides being an awesome teacher, dude had a point:

WE TEND TO OVERCOMPLICATE THINGS.

Don't feel bad if you do it, because it's human nature.

Multitasking is one way we make a mess of things.

Do you have friends who tell you they want to hang out, but rarely do? They mean well, but stuff always comes up. They are pulled in so many different directions, they end up forgetting or not having time. In reality, they get less done, because they try to do everything at once. They are a well meaning hot mess. Typically, they don't even realize it.

Basically, when you multitask you split your attention between different tasks and end up being less efficient and less productive.

Cardigan and suit wearing ninjas (psychologists and other scientists) have done experiments that showed:

1. Multitasking sucks (I read it in an article).
2. We get stuff done faster doing one task at a time compared to switching between tasks.
3. The more complex the tasks, the worse our performance and bigger the time waste when multitasking.

It's time to dump multitasking.

Help is on the way.

CHAPTER 11 – FOCUS OR DIE

Alright. Alright. You probably won't die if you continue to multitask, but just imagine if a knife juggler decided to text mom during one of his acts. Bad idea. Blood, fingers, eyeballs, possibly guts, everywhere!

Don't do that. Do this:

1. Stick to one task at a time.
2. Prioritize.
3. Use the Pomodoro Technique.

1.   ONE TASK AT A TIME

Focus on whatever you are studying or working on without distractions. Do not start a new task until you finish this one. Worst thing you can do is panic and start working on something else before the first task is done. What you will end up with is several things started, time used less efficiently, and a feeling of being overwhelmed.

On the other hand, if you get only one task done that day you are doing what many consistently fail to do. You are accomplishing goals. One at a time.

Put it in the WIN column.

2. PRIORITIZE

Chances are that on any given day you will have more than one school-related goal to accomplish. How do you begin?

Stay sane and pick just 3 most urgent things to do.

What if you feel like you have 10+ must do things?

Pick 3! Really.

Then, start with one of them. Work on this one task and only this one task without distractions until it is done.

Then, go to task #2. Finish it. Then #3. Same thing.

RESIST DISTRACTIONS AND SWITCHING BETWEEN YOUR 3 TASKS.

That might be tough to do: phone, social, random thoughts…

But, if you get all 3 done you are doing more than 97% of all students do, and even though I made up that statistic, it is probably (and sadly) true. You see, most students get so distracted and pulled in so many directions that they start a lot of things and finish few.

That might have been you before. But not any more.

Today, you get the WINNING FORMULA.

3. POMODORO

Pomodoro is a game changer, the winning formula. It is a simple technique that will change the way you study and work. It's so simple you may find it hard to believe it can do so much. No matter. It works.

Here it is:

1. **SET A TIMER TO 25 MINUTES.** Let everyone (Fam, BF, GF etc.) know what you are doing, so they don't interrupt or get upset if you don't respond to them.
2. **FOCUS ON ONE TASK.** Study. Write. Do math. Whatever. NO INTERRUPTIONS. No social media, gaming, texting etc.
3. **REWARD YOURSELF.** After successfully completing 25 minutes of hardcore awesomeness (studying etc.) do something you enjoy for 5 minutes and repeat the drill.

But check this out:

If 25 minutes seems too hard to start with, pick a shorter time period that is not so daunting. How does 15 minutes sound? Or 10? Even 5 minutes is better than 0.

The point is to start. Remember chapter 8? You have to train your brain first. Once you get rolling there'll be no stopping you!

Now you know. It's time to do.

ACTIONS:

1.   Do Pomodoro today.

Truth Bomb: If you say *"I'll try it,"* you won't do it. So from this day forward say instead: **"*I will do it.*"**

2.   Say It. Do It. Crush School.

CHAPTER 12 - DO IT NOW, SAVE TIME LATER

Remember how you were freaking out when you had sooo much stuff to do for school it was basically impossible?

Me too. The struggle is real.

Time is one of those things you can never get enough of, but you can learn how to spend less time freaking out and more time getting stuff done. Chances are, you'll still freak out from time to time, but at least it will be on your own terms.

In order for this to become your reality you must realize and apply this principle:

PUTTING THE TIME IN UPFRONT ACTUALLY SAVES TIME.

I'm not talking about procrastination here. What I'm saying is that you should do the many little things as you get the opportunity to do them, rather that wait to do them all at once. For example: Previewing a lecture will save you study time later, as those few well spent minutes will get your mind working on the topics and making connections right away.

I will talk about many other strategies throughout this book, which just as Previewing, take little time and effort, but pay off big.

These are things such as Summarizing or Taking Notes in the Margins.

They are strategies students often ignore not understanding their power. They don't get how going the extra inch now can help get them miles ahead, save time, and decrease stress later.

But not you. Not today. Not ever. You get it and you're ready.

CHAPTER 13 - PREVIEWING

Remember that movie preview you just saw?

Did it make you wonder how cool some parts of the movie will be?

Wasn't it awesome?

I'm hoping you answered: *Yes. Yes. Duh!*

Previewing is a very effective movie marketing strategy. It makes you think and it peaks interest. It's because your brain is looking for connections it already has and makes new connections related to the topic. Previewing awakens imagination so use it! And it's easy:

1. Before Reading: Read the chapter title and all of the headings and subheadings. Examine pictures, charts, graphs etc.
2. Lecture: If the presentation is available to you ahead of time take a few minutes to skim it. If not, but you know the topic, find it in the textbook or online and give it a quick look before class.

Previewing will do 3 awesome things for you:

1. Your brain will look for information it already has in storage on those topics before you read/listen.
2. You will know what's most important and focus on it more while reading/listening.
3. You will remember more of what you read/hear.

CHAPTER 14 - LEARN ACTIVELY

Active learning is all about staying uhm… active.

Whether during lectures, reading, discussions, or watching videos, the key to getting the most out of these activities is to keep your conscious mind involved.

For example you might just sit there and hear the teacher talk or mindlessly watch a video in class. You'll remember something, but not much. So if you really want to learn this stuff you have to do something with it.

You see, the most efficient way to learn is to use the information right away in several ways. You're already at school a third of each day, so you might as well use that time to save time later.

And when it's time to study for a test, there are better ways than repeatedly re-reading notes or chapters. The table on the next page lists passive and active learning activities in and out of the classroom.

Check it out!

FOCUS ON THE RIGHT SIDE.

Passive Learning	Active Learning
Waiting for the Teacher to Teach	Previewing Notes/Reading (Chapter 13)
Listening to Objectives	Writing Objectives Down
Watching a Lecture	Taking Notes During a Lecture (Chapter 27)
Copying Text Word for Word	Thinking About and Paraphrasing Text
Highlighting/Underlining Text	Taking Notes in the Margins (Chapter 25)
Putting the Notes Away Right Away	Summarizing the Notes
Re-reading Notes to Study	Recalling Notes (Chapter 15)
	Testing Yourself Asking Questions Making/Correcting Your Own Mistakes (Chapter 22)

And don't worry if some of the active learning activities are unclear right now. I will talk about them in the next chapters.

The key thing is that you know that in order to remember and understand what you are learning better, you have to allow your brain to process it and make meaning out of it. When you sit and stare at the teacher blankly or space out while reading a chapter, you're acting like a vegetable or a zombie.

There are many zombies walking around you. They sleepwalk through their classes hoping the information will magically seep into their brain. Then they complain when it doesn't. But not you. You learn actively, because zombies are only cool in movies. Or when they're in love.

CHAPTER 15 – ALWAYS SUMMARIZE

Even if you do nothing else do this: SUMMARIZE.

Don't get me wrong:

YOU SHOULD TAKE NOTES DURING LECTURES OR READING.

But if for some reason you don't, do yourself a huge favor and find it in your heart to summarize what you can remember from the learning experience.

I know. You might have a few minutes left at the end of class and want to catch up with your peeps. But you must resist.

SIT BACK DOWN AND WRITE DOWN THE KEY POINTS YOU LEARNED.

If you don't you will not remember.

What's the best way? The brain way, and because the brain can process only about 3 things at once focus on 3 things.

I know. Everything seemed important. Pick 3 things.

ACTIONS:

1. Skim your notes and pick 3 key topics covered.
2. Write a sentence or two for each topic.
3. SUPER IMPORTANT: Paraphrase and Combine Information.

If you didn't take notes (and this is painful for me to accept) dig deep and write down anything you can remember that your mind registered as important.

This will prove huge in the future.

CHAPTER 16 – BEAT PROCRASTINATION

Go ahead: Lie to yourself...

Convince yourself how successful you have been when you put things off to the last possible moment. And maybe you were at times. But guess what: YOU CAN DO BETTER. I know it. You know it.

SO WHY DO WE DO IT?

Most humans procrastinate. It's because our brain experiences what it reads as pain when it is about to be put to doing something difficult. In addition, the part of the brain responsible for rational thinking, the prefrontal cortex, gets tired easily.

In response, our brain looks for ways to stop these negative feelings and switches attention to something more pleasant. We do something else and start feeling happy, which is unfortunately only temporary, as the task we must do does not go away.

It's not easy, but

YOU CAN BEAT PROCRASTINATION.

Flip to the next page to see how.

5 BRAIN HACKS FOR BEATING PROCRASTINATION

1. Focus on the Process not the Product.

When studying, avoid thinking about how many pages you have to write or problems to solve as that brings on the pain that leads to procrastination.

Rather, calmly put the effort into doing the work.

There's no need to understand and finish everything in one session, so relax and break it up into smaller chunks.

2. Distractions will happen, so accept them and train yourself to move past them quickly.

Find a quiet space, use noise-cancelling headphones.

Short 5 minute breaks are actually good for your brain.

Just don't make them too long as that will make it hard to continue.

3. Plan: Write down 3-6 tasks you want to accomplish.

Do it the night before, so your mind starts working on them while you sleep. Plan your breaks and quitting time too.

It's okay if you did not finish all tasks if you gave it your best.

The goal is to make progress on (or complete) at least 3 of the tasks. Prioritize them in order of importance.

4. Trust in your new system and yourself.

Get support when you get stressed out or overwhelmed.

Ask friends who are successful to help out.

Talk to your parents, teachers, school counselors etc. and ask for help.

5. Use the Pomodoro Technique! (Chapter 11)

CHAPTER 17 - SPACE IT OUT

Got a big science test coming up? Or maybe a 50-word vocab quiz, because apparently your English teacher is insane?

Perhaps you filled out a study guide, made flashcards, or are using your notes to study. That's good! You want to do well and you're doing it right.

Now, let's

MAXIMIZE YOUR LEARNING BY SPACING IT OUT.

I'm not talking about daydreaming here, though I like it too.

In fact, I space out a lot. It drives my wife nuts.

What I am talking about is deciding how much time you want to devote to studying for the upcoming quiz or test and distributing it over several days (or weeks if you know that far in advance).

Let's look at a possible scenario.

It is Monday and you have a test on Friday. Normally, you might study for 3 hours the night before.

But what if you studied for 1 hour each on Monday and Tuesday, and 30 minutes each on Wednesday and Thursday?

You still get 3 hours of learning in, but now you've given your brain more time to absorb, process, and link information.

You were more focused, because you avoided looking at the same stuff for 3 hours straight.

And, you remember and understand more concepts and in greater depth now!

Awesomeness.

TIME IS A GAME CHANGER IN LEARNING. SPACE IT OUT.

But what if you don't have time?

You Hack Procrastination.

Huh? That's right. Hack Procrastination.

HACKING PROCRASTINATION

Twas the night before Test Day, when all through the house
Not a creature was stirring, not even a mouse.
The pages were spread on your desk with care,
In hopes that all knowledge would enter from there.

The others were nestled all snug in their beds,
While visions of Aced tests danced in their heads.
But your books, and your notes, and you thinking "Man!,"
Had just settled your brains for a last minute cram...

I am not advocating for the **Last Resort Tactic** I'm about to give you!

Do everything in your power to space your learning out over several days, or weeks if possible, because that's how you get your brain to remember and understand best.

But, if against my best advice, you ended up putting your studies off till the last possible moment, use the **CRUSH SCHOOL LAST RESORT CRAM TACTIC.**

CRUSH SCHOOL LAST RESORT CRAM TACTIC

1. Are you planning to study for 4 hours the night before a test? Don't.
2. Instead, study for 2 hours, go to sleep, and wake up 2 hours earlier the next day to study for 2 more hours.

Seems like it's all the same right?

Wrong!

Sure, you get the same amount of sleep and study time. But, by "sleeping on it" you're allowing time for your brain to process and link information. This makes stronger neural connections.

Studying after you sleep gives you a fresh look at the concepts and makes these neural connections even stronger!

The catch is that **If You Don't Sleep, None Of It May Matter.**

CHAPTER 18 - RECALL & MAKE LEARNING LAST

The learning strategy I talk about here will be a game changer for you. It is called RECALL and it's been around…

Problem is, most students re-read their notes, chapters, teacher presentations etc. over and over while studying for the test.

What they should be doing is recalling.

Let me ask you something:

Have you ever studied a lot by reading your notes or textbook over and over and still managed to do badly on a test? Did that leave you wondering why?

If so, the reason has to do with how you were studying.

You were re-reading not recalling.

SO WHAT IS RECALL AND WHY DOES IT WORK?

Thought you'd never ask!

Recall is retrieval of information from memory.

It is an active study strategy. Recall trumps re-reading (a passive way to study) because it results in deeper learning and better memory.

Research shows that recall is a more effective learning strategy than re-reading or concept-mapping.

WHY IS RECALL EFFECTIVE?

1. SEEING IS NOT BELIEVING. Students learn far more and on a deeper level when using recall because it involves "doing" and not just "seeing."

2. GAINING EXPERTISE. Retrieval from memory enhances more in-depth learning and brain chunk formation and linking.

3. MEMORY MAKING. Recall is a mental exercise that leads to formation of permanent memories so the learning sticks.

RECALL HACKS

 Test Yourself: This guards against the illusion of competence, which is you thinking you know, when you really don't (Chapter 22).

 Make Mistakes: Making mistakes while learning is good because it allows self correction and prevents test errors later (Chapter 20).

 Mix It Up: Recall in different places, environments, and situations to make information stick better (Chapter 19).

CORNELL NOTES ARE PERFECT FOR RECALL

 CORNELL NOTES COMPLEMENT RECALL. Cover the right side and only read the left side that contains trigger words, phrases, and questions.

Stretch your mind and try to remember as much as possible before you look at the right side. It's okay to peek if you gave it an honest try. Next time you will remember!

PRACTICE MAKES PERMANENT.

The more times you recall the
information you're learning, the
better you will understand and
remember it.

Doing this will make the neural
connections strong and lasting.
You won't just know it for the
test and quickly forget. The
knowledge will stay with you!

Everyone else re-reads, because they don't know any
better.

But not you.

YOU RECALL.

From now on, you stretch your brain. You make it
look for and find the information that's already
there.

And then you Crush School.

CHAPTER 19 - MIX IT UP

*"Don't hate the player; **change** the game."*

\- Steve Harvey

Changing things up when learning helps you learn better. It may be surprising, because we often rely on routines when we do certain things. But if you're studying for a test, mixing it up may be just what the doctor ordered.

WHAT you study, WHERE you study, and HOW you study helps your brain form stronger connections. When you mix it up the information is stored in different parts of your brain.

The result? You remember, understand, and use information better.

Remember Learning Styles (Chapter 3)? The more ways in which you are exposed to the information, the better you remember and understand it.

It's because your brain will store what you learn in many places. That leads to more neural connections. And connections are where it's at!

BENEFITS OF MIXING IT UP

Mixing Up What, How, and Where You Study Increases

Mixing Up What, How, and Where You Study Increases

Mixing Up What, How, and Where You Study Increases

MEMORY RETENTION

UNDERSTANDING

SCHOOL SUCCESS

MIX UP WHAT YOU LEARN

Jump back and forth between different concepts or problems instead of finishing one topic or one kind of a problem and moving on to the next.

Alternate more difficult problems with easier ones.

This will prevent boredom and keep your mind more alert and focused. You can also alternate between subjects when studying for finals. Just make sure you don't leave things unfinished.

MIX UP HOW YOU LEARN

 Use many study strategies when learning. After re-reading notes, practice recalling them. Write summaries of learning experiences such as reading, lectures, and videos. Quiz yourself on the material. Teach it to others. Form study groups.

This will store the information in different parts of your brain and form stronger neural pathways improving memory and understanding.

MIX UP WHERE YOU LEARN

 Study in different places. If you mainly study at home, try a cafe or the library for a change.
When at home study at your desk, on the couch, on your bed, or outside. If you lose focus, change your learning environment.

This helps you deal with unexpected circumstances. Your brain will be better prepared for any "curve balls" thrown at you. You'll be less stressed and more successful.

CHAPTER 20 - FAILURE IS THE ONLY OPTION

"Stay hungry. Stay foolish." - Steve Jobs

Failure is the only option?

What?!?!

Isn't this book supposed to help you crush school, not fail it?

Yes it is. Chill. The failure I'm talking about is of the good variety, because it helps you succeed.

Take Steve Jobs. He was a pretty successful and brilliant dude. Where would we be without iTunes, smartphones, and tablets? Steve's success though was mainly a result of his attitude toward failure. While brilliant, he failed at Apple the first time around and resigned in 1985. He came back again in 1997 and lead the company out of bankruptcy to the awesomeness that it is today.

Oh, and after first leaving Apple, he founded Pixar and revolutionized movie animation, because he could. He then came back to Apple and crushed it.

How did Steve do it?

1. He failed a lot.
2. Instead of crying about it, he learned from his failures.

The path to greatness is filled with failure and only those who take risks, fail, and learn from their mistakes achieve it.

Truth Bomb: Many students are afraid to make mistakes, so they don't take enough risks in school.

As a result, they never learn to fail forward.

FAILING FORWARD

"I can accept failure, everyone fails at something. But I can't accept not trying."

- Michael Jordan aka the G.O.A.T.

Failing forward is understanding that

FAILING DOES NOT MAKE YOU A FAILURE.

If you see yourself as a failure, you will be a failure. This is because you are training your brain to accept you as a failure. And failure behaviors follow.

To be successful, you need to change how you view failure.

So, read, accept, believe, and live these truths:

1. **Failure is tough. It's also unavoidable. I accept it will happen to me and I plan to learn from it.**
2. **Failure is temporary, so I will take risks.**
3. **Everyone fails, but successful people like me view failure as the beginning, not the end.**
4. **The more I fail, the more I succeed.**

Check out the next page for a couple of examples of how the right approach to failure can help you become a better learner.

RANDOM DAY IN CLASS: Teacher asks a question.

OPTION 1: You don't answer. You think you may know it, but don't want to be wrong. You often forget the answer the teacher gave to her own question.

OPTION 2: You answer. You get it wrong. The teacher corrects you. You remember it and you answer 5 questions related to it right on the test.

ANALYSIS: It doesn't take a genius to figure out that OPTION #2 is better. But why?

Mostly, it has to do with the fact that when you fail to answer correctly, your mind remembers the answer given as a correction.

Also, you might have felt a little embarrassed speaking up and being wrong. Your brain remembers the feeling associated with this event and makes more neural connections. Thus, you remember and learn better.

FINAL THOUGHTS ON FAILURE

Whether in class or studying at home, never tell yourself "I Don't Know."

At the very least, attempt to answer the question, define the word, or explain the concept. If you're really struggling, say something connected to it. Be wrong now, so you can be right later. Fail forward.

Truth Bomb: When you say "I Don't Know" you tell your brain "Don't Learn This."

I'm not ready to accept that. Are you?

CHAPTER 21 - TEAM UP

"The first principle is that you must not fool yourself and you are the easiest person to fool."

– Richard Feynman

Why is it a good idea to work in a group?

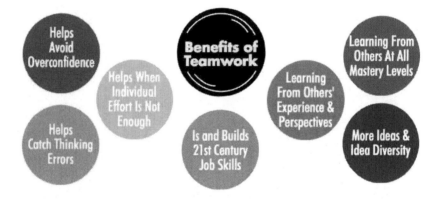

Bottom Line: Whether you like it or not you will have to work well with people in the future.

Even if you become the boss you'll have to collaborate, rather than boss others around.

Doing it the old school way gets you the middle finger and a "see ya!" in the world of today.

Resisting teamwork is normal. It's because our brain focuses on survival and automatically fears trusting others. But you must remember that this is the new age and the likelihood of getting our skull cracked with a club is very low.

Besides, we have a tendency to "fill in the blanks" or create "understandings" that are false when we don't know or fear something. Collaboration helps you avoid such nonsense.

STUDY GROUPS

It's always a good idea to get a study group going on your own. It's an awesome way to be proactive.

This is how you become a better leader. You organize when, where, and how. You get others on board. You keep yourself and others committed. You study, teach, and learn from each other.

Keep your study group small. 3 to 4 people is ideal. Pick people who can focus and help you learn. Be honest with yourself. Will you be productive if you work with your best friend? Yes? Maybe? Not really?

You can meet before or after school in the school library, or Starbucks, or somebody's house.

Chances are that if you organize it in your house, your mom will get you snacks or bake a cake – she'll be so proud of you taking control of your learning. And she'll want to support you 100%.

It will score you some serious points with dad too, which will come in handy when it's time to ask for those car keys or a different perk.

But don't tell them I told you. Just let it happen.

When forming a study group it's important to understand that effective teamwork doesn't just happen.

Good teamwork habits have to be formed and developed so that group goals are accomplished and everyone in the group benefits from participation in it.

And the best way to get good at collaboration is to do it.

Check this out.

There are times when I see a student contribute little to the group. For example, the "group manager" might skip out on intellectual work.

That's a real bummer, because this is where all of the action happens!

Being involved in the brainstorming and decision making is how you best learn content and collaboration.

So don't be "just" the "manager." Become a mastermind.

CRUSH SCHOOL! MASTERMINDS

The #1 purpose of a Mastermind group is to help all group members achieve success. How?

1. You have clear goals and agenda when you meet.
2. You brainstorm and learn together.
3. You are honest, respectful, and compassionate.
4. You hold yourself and everyone else accountable.
5. You support one another.

BUILDING AN EFFECTIVE MASTERMIND GROUP

TEAM CULTURE

- "In This Together"
  - Common Goals

SAFETY, SUPPORT, GROWTH

- Mutual Respect
- Openness (No Idea Is Dumb)
- Taking Risks Encouraged
- Feedback, Not Criticizing

HIGH EXPECTATIONS

- Set Rules & Norms
- Everyone Contributes
- Everyone Is Accountable

TIME

- It Takes Time To Click
- Hiccups Happen
- Keep Team Together
- Be Consistent

CHAPTER 22 – TEST YOURSELF

Testing yourself is one of the best study strategies you can use when preparing for quizzes and tests. It's also great presentation prep. Chances are you will be asked questions. Prepping for questions in advance will help you think on your feet and not choke when it's go time.

 ## HOW DO YOU TEST YOURSELF?

Write questions about the material you're studying. Challenge yourself while at it. It's okay to write a few "What is" questions. Just remember that asking: "What is a cat?" leads to a response that only describes what Mr. Furball is.

As you progress from grade to grade your teachers will challenge you more. They'll ask fewer "What is" questions and more questions that cause you to go deeper into the concepts.

That's a good thing! It teaches you to start using what you're learning; becoming smarter.

Let's talk chemistry.

Whether you love or hate it, you'll have to study to do well in chem. Not just study though.

YOU'LL HAVE TO STUDY SMART.

One way to do that is to ask good questions.

For example, you can ask: "What is an atom?"

It's a fair question and not a horrible one. Thing is though, it only tells you to look at the basics. And basics don't get no excellents.

A better question, one that causes you to gain a deeper understanding is: "What role do atoms play in the Universe?" or "Compare the size of the atom and its particles to something we can actually see."

Now you have to dig deep. Find out more. Force your mind to make new connections. Really understand it.

And that's how you crush it.

So do it.

Write DEEP questions. Answer them. Test yourself. Learn like a boss. Crush School.

CHAPTER 23 - TEACH IT

If you can teach something you really understand it.

Think about it. Could you explain to a 5
year old what your favorite musical artist,
sport, or hobby is all about?

Sure you could. You'd be able to give a lot
of information with all kinds of details.
It's because you studied it a lot.

Let me tell you a secret about teachers.

We are sometimes put in situations in which
to teach something we are not very comfortable
teaching. We might not have taught it in a long time
or never taught it. But now, for whatever reason,
the principal asks us to teach it.

And we do.

And we kill it.

So how do we teach something that's pretty new to
us?

Thought you'd never ask!

HOW TEACHERS TEACH SOMETHING NEW

1. We read about it.
2. We watch videos on the topic.
3. We think about it and draw pictures in our heads.
4. If it involves math, we solve all types of problems to make sure we understand and can teach them.
5. We ask other teachers for explanations and ideas.
6. We create presentations on it.
7. We create assignments on it.
8. We write lesson plans (aka teacher cheat sheets), which have notes to help us remember what to do and how to do it.
9. When it's go time, we kill it!

And you can do the same. Prepare like a teacher does, then teach it. When you do, you kill it too.

CHAPTER 24 - STOP. THINK. REFLECT.

"What were you thinking?!?!"

Have you ever been on the receiving end of such statements? I have. It was the statement my parents often used after I already did something rash, or dumb, or both. The answer was always "I Don't Know."

We are beings driven by survival. We react to situations or events quickly. We might not have the chance to consider all the reaction choices. Our brains do what they evolved to do. They react quickly and the reactions are meant to protect us from threats.

Problem is, things that were threats thousands or even hundreds of years ago are no longer threats today...

Being able to sit down and really think was difficult 20,000 years ago. If you weren't paying attention to your surroundings you became sabretooth dinner or got knocked in the head with a club of a jealous caveman wanting your woman. And the cave ladies knew how to throw a mean rock as well.

Luckily, it's unlikely to get clubbed these days, so **TURN YOUR MIND ON**

Because the human mind travels like 1000 miles per second, you have to intentionally stop it to reflect.

While teachers teach you to think, most of them focus on the subject and teach you to think about it. That's good, but how do you use the subject to enter the world of your inner mind?

First, you must understand how your brain learns. Then, you turn your brain on. You start thinking about your thinking.

Here's an example. A physics teacher might tell you that electricity is like water in a pipe. Turning the faucet on is like hooking up the battery to a light bulb. Opening the faucet makes water flow. The battery makes current flow. That's a great analogy!

But here's the thing. As they are pressured to cover the curriculum, many teachers might not have the time to tell you to COME UP WITH SUCH ANALOGIES AND CONNECTIONS YOURSELF.

Here are a few other Jedi Mind Tricks you can use while learning:

1. When reading, stop and consider what it brings to mind and what feelings the author is evoking.
2. When listening to a presentation or watching a video, pause it and connect the concepts to something you know.
3. Create a metaphor that helps you remember a concept.
4. If you're not sure you're making the right connections, ask your teacher.

SELF REFLECTION

When you're learning, think of things you know or might have experienced that connect to the topic. Think of things that are similar to it. Think of how it relates to you, others, and the world. Think of ways you can use it. When you do that, you find meaning. Finding meaning is reflecting.

Reflection is a conscious process. It's a skill which, if perfected, will help you become truly present. You will be more aware of other people's feelings and what impact your words and actions have on people. You will be amazed by the hidden things you notice as events happen and when you reflect on them later.

You can reflect in your mind, but reflection is best done through writing. Get a journal and start writing about stuff that happens in your life. If someone says something that speaks to you, capture it. Then, explain it. Write down your ideas, questions, and realizations.

The skill of self reflection develops through constant practice. When you reflect, you repeatedly enter the world of your mind. You constantly find new truths, understandings, and epiphanies there. Start reflecting and you will start operating in the world most people don't even know exists.

So drop the old programming and write the new code.

Stop. Think. Reflect.

CHAPTER 25 - READING TIPS

Yes! To crush school YOU WILL HAVE TO READ. Reading is often the difference between the haves and the have nots; those who succeed and those who are stuck in the same place.

To be able to take a piece of text, extract it's teachings, and apply them in many contexts is true power. It's the sort of power that gives rise to ideas, creativity, and innovation.

And, it helps you crush school too.

Let's talk movies for a bit. Ever notice how when you watch a movie the second time you find that you missed some things? Reading is the same way, so commit to reading whatever you're reading at least two times.

YOU HAVE TO READ A PIECE OF TEXT MORE THAN ONCE TO GET MUCH OF THE INFO.

And, if you *actively* read the same text the third time, you will notice that you get more out of it still. The tips coming up will help you get really good at remembering and understanding. Ready?

HAVE A SYSTEM = GET THE INFO.

I don't know about you, but I often space out when I read. It's not that the book is boring. Sometimes I get into the reading and start analyzing what the author says in my mind. And my mind goes places. All of a sudden, I catch myself reading the words on the page, but thinking about Scarlett Johannson.

Does that happen to you? If it does, here's a trick you can use to keep focus and get the info.

WRITE IN THIS BOOK.

What?!?! But, my teacher said… Blah! Blah! Blah! Don't worry. I don't give detention and you won't owe me $87.50 for damaging the book.

IT'S YOUR BOOK, SO USE IT TO HELP YOU.

Yeah. I know it's pretty and all, but still

MARK IT UP!

When you do that, you focus better, remember more, and can find the most important stuff quicker the next time, which builds up your understanding. Check it out!

CRUSH SCHOOL! READING TIPS:

1. Underline or highlight key statements in each paragraph. This is the important stuff, not the info that supports the main points.
2. You are probably overdoing it if you highlight/underline more than ⅓ of the page. Just sayin'...
3. When you read a section the second time, take a few notes in the margins on WHY WHAT YOU READ IS IMPORTANT. Process, then write.
4. Next time you come back to the text, focus on recalling and writing deep study questions on the underlined information and margin notes.
5. If you absolutely can't mark up the text take Cornell Notes on Steroids.

CHAPTER 26 – WRITE IT DOWN OR PERISH

Did you ever have a great idea pop in your head and it was so good that you knew you'd remember it no matter what?

The story probably went something like this:

Seemingly out of nowhere a great idea popped in your head. You went about your day, but later thought about having this great idea. When you tried to remember what it actually was, you realized that you FORGOT. Just like that. Gone. Forever.

That's a bummer. So, next time you have a great idea,

WRITE IT DOWN SO YOU CAN REMEMBER IT.

This is why you should take notes in class. You might be one of those people who remember stuff well when they hear or see it. That's awesome! But, and be 100% honest with yourself here, do you remember all of the important stuff all the time?

Probably not…

Scientists say that students who write notes down on paper learn more than students who use laptops.

I don't know if it's the same if you use an iPad, but I think using Sketchnoting is an awesom ~e idea.

Handwriting usually takes longer than typing, so students develop strategies that help them be more efficient. Doing so requires brain processing that leads to increased concept comprehension.

I prefer pen and paper, but not everyone agrees. One thing's for sure though: Taking notes trumps doing nothing. And, you can take awesomer (totally a word) notes than ever before.

CHAPTER 27 – AWESOMER NOTES

"Don't worry about never having time to write. Just write what you can in the time you do have and give yourself a big clap on the back, followed by a double latte and a blueberry muffin."

– Rachel Johnson

Whether you prefer taking notes on paper or digitally, to get the most out of notes, you want to make the process an active one. Many students copy word for word when taking notes. There may be good reasons why, but this simple truth remains:

YOU LEARN VERY LITTLE WHEN YOU COPY WORD FOR WORD.

It's because you don't engage your mind. Not really… When you copy verbatim, all you're doing is mindlessly writing stuff down on paper or on a device. You're not thinking about the meaning of the words. And, your brain doesn't get the chance to properly process the information. And guess what?

UNPROCESSED INFO IS GIBBERISH.

Why would anyone want to fill their mind with gibberish?

So how do you engage your mind more? Well… Ladies and Gentlemen, I give you

THE 7 COMPONENTS OF AWESOME NOTES

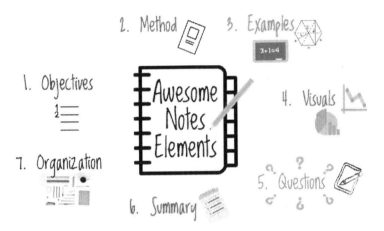

Here's the deal:

1. **Objectives:** Learning objectives tell you what you are supposed to learn. Always write them down.

2. **Method:** Develop and use the same way to take notes. Your brain will like the familiarity and be more efficient.

3. **Examples:** Write down examples when they're given. They put the ideas in easier contexts and improve memory.

4. **Visuals:** Represent major concepts with visuals. Your brain processes them more effectively than text alone.

5. **Questions:** Write down questions you have when learning. If you can't ask them now, you can find answers later.

6. **Summary:** Spending 3-5 minutes summarizing help your brain remember more and will pay off big on future projects, quizzes, and tests.

7. **Organization:** Neat and organized notes make finding info easy and your brain sees it as less of a pain to study.

It may not be possible to always do everything. Just know this: **The more effort you put in, the better the results.**

CHAPTER 28 - CREATIVITY IS A SUPERWEAPON

Effective Car Commercials: Now every time I pass a KIA "Soul" in the street I'm disappointed the driver is not a Hamster.

— Neil deGrasse Tyson

Creativity allows you to create. Everyone has the potential to create, but sadly not everyone knows it. The hard truth is that

CREATIVITY IS OFTEN KILLED AT SCHOOL AND LATER AT WORK.

Taking the creative way often requires going against your protective brain. This means taking risks and sometimes taking the more difficult path. Light bulb moments often happen outside of your comfort zone. Step out of it and believe that

YOU ARE CREATIVE EVEN IF YOU'RE NOT THE ARTSY-FARTSY TYPE.

Creativity is a Superweapon that makes Superheroes out of those who dare to seize it. So Seize It. Become more creative. When you do, coming up with ideas in school will become easier. You will become an awesome problem solving innovation machine.

Problem solving is what school, work, and life are all about.

THERE ARE THINGS YOU CAN DO TO BECOME MORE CREATIVE.

Take a peek at

 GETTING CREATIVE

1. You Must Have The DRIVE TO CREATE.

If you're not motivated to do something, you will struggle completing it and your creativity will suffer. Bring your mind's focus to the rewards of the project, not the risks and difficulties it presents.

Motivation can be increased by creating a calm, soft, and relaxing work environment and staying positive.

2. You Must THINK TO CREATE.

Observe and think through the problem. Brainstorm, generate, and eliminate a lot of ideas. Accept wild and crazy ideas. They can lead to light bulb moments even if they don't work. Try to use concepts and experiences from other areas/subjects.

3. You Must COMBINE TO CREATE.

Build an idea bank in your brain by being open to and learning many different things and subjects. Combine these concepts to form new ideas. Seeing an elephant riding a Harley in your head may be crazy, but sure is creative. It's hard to forget too.

The bigger your brain library is, the more creative you are. The more diverse your knowledge, the more you can innovate.

Work in teams and combine ideas. Teamwork teaches you to look at problems from many angles and new perspectives. Check out Chapter 21 for ideas on how to form effective teams and how to get the most out of collaboration.

4. You Must WORK TO CREATE.

Plan your work and work your plan. Good habits allow you to focus on being creative. Work hard, but build in some breaks. "A-has" often occur when intensity is followed by relaxation.

Use the "Show Me" approach. Don't shut down any ideas! Build and play with prototypes to prove or disprove designs.

Learn from mistakes and failures. Analyze why an idea or prototype failed. Apply this knowledge to future solutions.

5. You Must COMMIT TO CREATE.

Maintain focus and avoid distractions. Multitasking slows progress down and shows lack of organization.

Formulate goals. Knowing what you want and making progress motivates you to keep going.

Accept that failure and rejection will happen. Learn from them and move on to stay motivated.

Remember that **Nothing Happens In One Giant Leap**. The solution will take a series of well thought through steps, hard work, and perseverance. Believe It!

Truth Bomb: CREATIVITY is a result of the CONSTANT DRIVE TOWARD GOALS, achieved through THINKING, HARD WORK, COMMITMENT, and COMBINATION OF DIFFERENT CONCEPTS.

CHAPTER 29 - NEVER EVER GIVE UP

"Once you stop learning you start dying."

– Einstein

Truth Bomb: Most students give up on learning a tough concept before their brain has a chance to understand it.

Many give up after only the first time they tried to learn something. They don't get it right away and think they're not smart enough. Others might understand on the spot so some think they're smart.

But, in reality the "smart ones" already have some knowledge on the topic before it's talked about, even if they don't realize it! Crazy, right?

Not really. Each encounter with the information you try to learn, or topics related to it, allows your brain to grow.

So,

EVEN IF YOU DON'T GET IT THE FIRST, SECOND, OR FIFTH TIME TRUST YOURSELF THAT YOU WILL AND YOU WILL.

Not because of the Dark Arts (though I think Severus Snape was cool), but because your brain needs time to make neural connections that will help it understand difficult concepts.

In fact, the time in between is sometimes more important than the time when you study.

Your brain works overtime!

Actually, it never stops working, so it is connecting the pieces while you are playing ball, eating muffins, or sleeping. The important part is time.

GIVE YOUR BRAIN TIME.

Others may give up on themselves, because they do not understand how the brain learns. But not you. Not anymore. You get it and you crush it.

CHAPTER 30 - CHILLAX

"Where your mind goes, energy flows."

– Ernest Holmes

Getting to this chapter means one of two things:

1. You are either drinking the Kool-Aid, which means you are well on your way to becoming an awesome learner.
   or
2. You are OCD.

I hope #1 is true for you, because I'm about to tell you to do some weird stuff.

Well… I thought some of it was weird when I was a teen, but the world has come a long way. Your generation is way more open and accepting of the weird, which is cool. Respect.

Anyways. Stress kills. Literally. It shortens your life, by causing all kinds of health issues.

In addition to experiencing health problems, people tend to fall into bad habits, such as putting things off, addiction, and vegging out on the couch when they feel stressed. Stress often affects sleep, which can affect school success.

Basically, Stress Sucks! And while you can't kill stress completely, you can control it.

Do you wanna know how?

5 CRUSH SCHOOL WAYS TO CHILLAX

1. Meditate:

If someone told me I should meditate when I was in middle school or high school I'd think they've been smoking something. But, while meditation might seem to be for hippies and Buddhists, and a weird waste of time, 5 minutes of quietly sitting down and listening to yourself breathe (weird I know) can actually help you decrease stress and increase awareness.

Just saying.

2. **Exercise:**

This one's really important. Physical activity is key to new neuron formation and neuron survival and it improves memory. If you're not a sporty type you might resist this one.

I totally get it.

So do whatever. Anything to get moving. Take walks with your dog or friends. Ride a bike. Rock climb. Mow the lawn. Jump on the bed 43 times every day.

I don't care what you do. Just move!

3. **Sleep:**

Getting enough sleep keeps your body and mind fresh and decreases stress. Remember Chapter 9? Toxins floating around? Tired and irritated brain?

Who needs that?

4. **Talk To Yourself:**

No, not out loud when you're at the mall or on the bus. That's super weird.

Use POSITIVE SELF TALK in your mind or when alone. It's less weird that way, and it helps you deal with negative emotions. It's very useful before a big test or presentation you are stressing over.

Tell yourself that you've got this and that you will kill it. When you do that, your brain does everything it can to make that reality.

So if you tell yourself you will do badly… Nah. That's not happening! Just make sure you prepare well, so your brain actually contains the information you need.

5. Breathe:

Sure. If you're reading this you have no choice but to breathe. That's not what I'm talking about. What I'm saying is that there will be stressful times, like tests and presentations, when you should turn the breathing autopilot off and control it.

Slow it down. Relax your muscles. Draw deep belly breaths and exhale.

Relaxation will boost your energy, focus, productivity, and problem-solving.

GET IT DONE YO!

KEEP CALM AND CRUSH SCHOOL

You have all the tools you need now. Use them.

The key message of this book is that the more times and ways you process the information the better you will remember and learn it.

Even if you use a couple of strategies given here CONSISTENTLY you will see improvement in your learning and performance at school, but

CONSISTENCY IS THE KEY.

Improvement is cool, but I want you to CRUSH IT. That's why I wrote this thing. So, make a plan to learn and use as many strategies as you can.

COMMIT TO YOUR PLAN BY WRITING IT ALL DOWN.

But, do it gradually.

No need to do it all at once. If you try, you may
be setting yourself up for disappointment. Too much
to do overwhelms your mind and you shut down.

One at a time works.

One at a time is easy.

Just keep learning and applying.

*"It doesn't matter how slowly you go as long as you
don't stop"* - Confucius

Trust Yourself. You Have the Power. Use It.

BONUS #1 — CORNELL NOTES ON STEROIDS

Hey! Just in case you hadn't had enough info or tools to use I thought I might give you one more. You might have heard of Cornell Notes, but have you heard of Cornell Notes On Steroids? That's right. These notes are jacked!

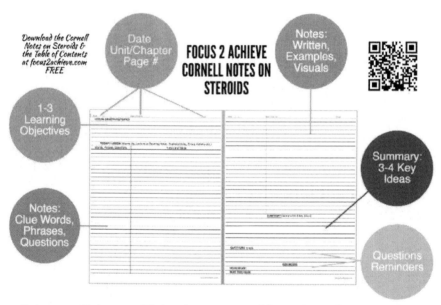

I know. I know. This is too small and useless.

Check out how to get the full size template on the next page.

You can get the pages to hole punch and stick in your binder at www.focus2achieve.com/focus-method-notes

Or, you can buy the Cornell Notes On Steroids Notebook. Use the code **CrushSchoolSale** for a 30% discount available only to those who buy and read this book. It comes in black, purple, or blue and contains the Cornell Notes on Steroids Template.

You can get it at focus2achieve.com/products

BONUS #2 - CRUSH TESTS!

Hey #2! One bonus just isn't enough. At least not for me. You got this far. You read this thing. In my book, you're the bomb and I want to give you one more thing.

I want to give you the Crush Tests Checklist I've developed, so that you can have a game changing tool that helps you prepare for tests and exams.

Get the free download here → http://bit.ly/2c4ZVb4

I put it on the next page so you can see why it rocks.

Print it.

Follow the directions on it.

Crush Tests.

Crush School.

CRUSH THAT TEST CHECKLIST

Check "Yes" only if you did the things described always or often (as opposed to occasionally or never).

DO EVERYTHING IN YOUR POWER TO ANSWER "YES" TO EVERY QUESTION.

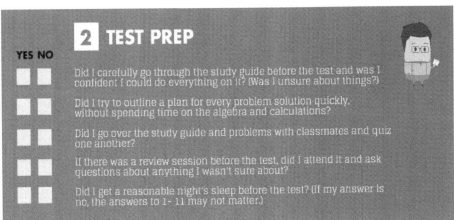

1 LEARNING (CLASS/HOME)

YES NO

Did I make a serious effort to understand the material?
(Re-reading notes and looking at problem examples does not count!)

Did I work with classmates on problem solving?
(Looking at them doing problems does not count!)

Did I try to outline a plan for every problem solution before asking for help and working with classmates? (What steps should I take?)

Did I participate actively in group work and discussions?
(Contributing ideas, asking questions)

Did I talk with the teacher when I was having trouble with something?
(Did I ask for help?)

Did I understand ALL homework/classwork problem solutions when I handed them in? (Did I know where the answers came from?)

Did I ask in class for explanations of homework/classwork problem solutions that weren't clear to me?

2 TEST PREP

YES NO

Did I carefully go through the study guide before the test and was I confident I could do everything on it? (Was I unsure about things?)

Did I try to outline a plan for every problem solution quickly, without spending time on the algebra and calculations?

Did I go over the study guide and problems with classmates and quiz one another?

If there was a review session before the test, did I attend it and ask questions about anything I wasn't sure about?

Did I get a reasonable night's sleep before the test? (If my answer is no, the answers to 1- 11 may not matter.)

Use the checklist above as a reminder of how to learn and study throughout each unit of study in every class. The more "Yeses" you check, the better prepared you will be for the test. If you check 2 or more "Nos", consider making some changes in how you learn and prepare for the next test.

Credit: Adapted for K-12 from the Test Preparation Checklist for Engineering Students by Prof. Richard M. Felder of North Carolina State University- http://www4.ncsu.edu/unity/lockers/users/f/felder/public/Columns/memo.pdf

REFERENCES

Ashton, Steven (2015). How to Fly a Horse: The Secret History of Creation, Invention, and Discovery. Random House LLC.

Beeman, Mark & Kounios, John (2015). The Eureka Factor: Aha Moments, Creative Insight, and the Brain. Random House LLC.

Bartow, T., Rudy, M., & Selk, J (2015). Organize Tomorrow Today: 8 Ways to Retrain Your Mind to Optimize Performance at Work and in Life. De Capo Lifelong Books.

Carey, benedict (2015). How We Learn: The Surprising Truth About When, Where, and Why It Happens. Random House LLC.

Chick, Nancy. Learning Styles. Vanderbilt University.

Doolittle, Peter (2013). How your working memory makes sense of the world. TEDGlobal 2013 Talk.

Felder, Richard. Test Preparation Checklist for Engineering Students. North Carolina State University.

Guise, Stephen (2013). Mini Habits: Smaller Habits, Bigger Results.

Kelley, David & Kelley, Tom (2013). <u>Creative Confidence: Unleashing the Creative Potential Within Us All.</u> Random House LLC.

Oakley, Barbara & Sejnowski, Terrence (2015). <u>Learning How To Learn: Powerful mental tools to help you master tough subjects</u>. University of California, San Diego.

Pashler, Harold, McDaniel, M., Rohrer, D., & Bjork, R. (2008). <u>Learning styles: Concepts and evidence</u>. *Psychological Science in the Public Interest*. 9.3 103-119.

Shook, Lori & Svensen, Frode (2015). <u>Team Up!: Applying Lessons from Neuroscience to Improve Collaboration, Innovation and Results.</u> Shooksvensen ltd.

van Aalderen, Sandra (2015). <u>Teachers, know your brain!</u>. TEDxAmsterdamED Talk 2015.

Wardlow, Liane. <u>The Science Behind Better Collaboration and Student Groupings and Technology.</u> Pearson Research Network.